DISCOVERING
ANCIENT CIVILIZATIONS

THE
INCAS

David West

Gareth Stevens
PUBLISHING

Please visit our website, www.garethstevens.com.
For a free color catalog of all our high-quality books,
call toll free 1-800-542-2595 or fax 1-877-542-2596.

Cataloging-in-Publication Data

Names: West, David.
Title: The Incas / David West.
Description: New York : Gareth Stevens Publishing, 2017. | Series: Discovering ancient civilizations | Includes index.
Identifiers: ISBN 9781482450514 (pbk.) | ISBN 9781482450538 (library bound) | ISBN 9781482450521 (6 pack)
Subjects: LCSH: Incas–Juvenile literature. | Indians of South America–Andes Region–Juvenile literature.
Classification: LCC F3429.W47 2017 | DDC 980'.013–dc23

First Edition

Published in 2017 by
Gareth Stevens Publishing
111 East 14th Street, Suite 349
New York, NY 10003

Copyright © 2017 David West Books

Designed by David West Books

Printed in the United States of America

CPSIA compliance information: Batch #CS16GS: For further information contact Gareth Stevens, New York, New York at 1-800-542-2595.

DISCOVERING
ANCIENT CIVILIZATIONS

THE
INCAS

David West

Gareth Stevens
PUBLISHING

CONTENTS

SAPA INCA RULED AN EMPIRE

Inca is the word we use to describe the Andean tribe and all the people that they conquered. They were a small tribe who built their capital, Cuzco, in 1300. Under three consecutive rulers they expanded their empire by conquering the other Andean tribes. By 1525 they had carved out an empire that extended for 2,500 miles (4,023 km).

The Inca rulers were known as **Sapa Inca** and were regarded as gods. All the land and people belonged to the ruler.

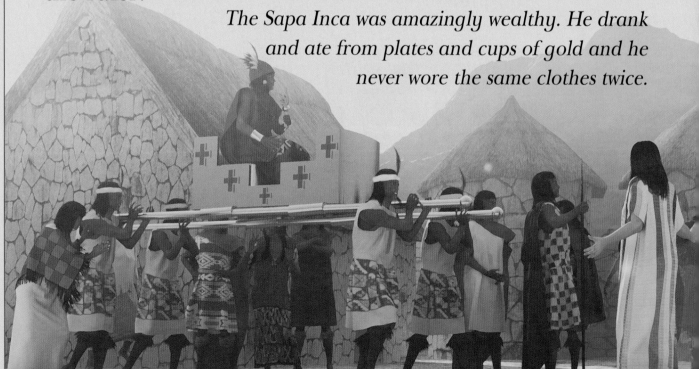

The Sapa Inca was amazingly wealthy. He drank and ate from plates and cups of gold and he never wore the same clothes twice.

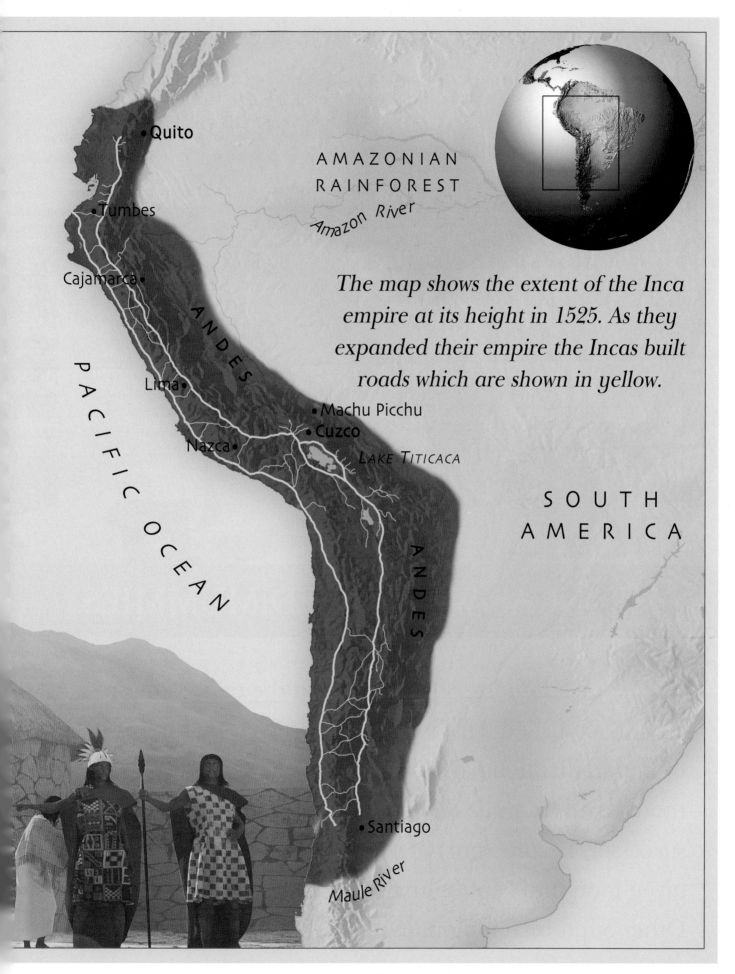

QUITO

AMAZONIAN
RAINFOREST

Amazon River

The map shows the extent of the Inca empire at its height in 1525. As they expanded their empire the Incas built roads which are shown in yellow.

Tumbes

Cajamarca

ANDES

PACIFIC OCEAN

Lima

Nazca

Machu Picchu

Cuzco

LAKE TITICACA

SOUTH
AMERICA

ANDES

Santiago

Maule River

THE INCAS WORSHIPED MUMMIES

When the Sapa Inca died the entire empire mourned. His body was preserved by the process of **mummification**. He was not thought to be dead, though. All his male descendants, except for the chosen successor, became part of the dead Inca's court. He was given food and kept in luxury as if he was still alive. Other Sapa Inca mummies were even taken to visit him.

8

Royal mummies are paraded in front of the Sapa Inca during the religious Festival of the Dead.

All the lands of the Incas still belonged to the dead Sapa Inca. This meant that the new Sapa Inca had to build his own palace and conquer new lands for himself.

Most mummies dried naturally in the dry, cold air of the Andes.

THE INCAS HAD A MASSIVE ARMY

When Inca Pachacuti became ruler of the Incas in 1438 he started expanding their territory. He led the army on successful expeditions against the other tribes that were dotted amongst the rugged landscape of the Andes. After each conquest the Inca army grew. At the height of the empire the army had grown to approximately 200,000 men.

*Using **maces** and slings, an invading Inca army overwhelms a small force of tribal warriors.*

New tribes were absorbed into the empire. Those that resisted were conquered. The Incas forced their new people to follow the Inca way of life. The plundered goods were sent back to Cuzco.

Warriors fought mainly with maces although slings, spears, and axes were sometimes used as well.

THE INCAS BUILT USING GIANT ROCKS

The Incas built many of their buildings using large stones cut to fit together precisely. No **mortar** was used and the fit was so accurate that even a thin knife could not be slid between the stones. Some cut blocks, such as those at the fortress Saksaywaman weighed more than 150 tons (136 tonnes).

Inca warriors gather along the ramparts of the fortress, Saksaywaman, which was built on a hillside overlooking Cuzco.

Inca buildings were usually rectangular and built from local stones. Some have been preserved in places like Machu Picchu.

Situated on a mountain ridge, Machu Picchu was built around 1450 as an estate for the Inca emperor Pachacuti.

INCA ROADS STRETCHED OVER 15,000 MILES

The Incas had no wheeled transport or horses, so everybody had to travel by foot. They traveled on an amazing road system built across jungles, deserts, swamps, and along the edges of steep ravines. The main Inca highway was the "Royal Road," which ran 1,400 miles (2,253 km) from Cuzco to Quito. To cross deep ravines engineers built **suspension bridges**.

Merchants cross a suspension bridge that spans a deep ravine. Steps have been cut into the cliff face as part of the road.

The roads were the arteries of the Inca empire. Armies traveled on them to conquer new lands. Messengers, merchants, and nobles also used them but commoners had to get special permission to travel on them.

Relays of running messengers, known as chasqui, could cover 150 miles (240 km) per day on these roads.

INCAS FARMED ON TERRACES

Much of the land was mountainous and difficult to farm. Farmers cut into the hillside and built stone walls to create terraces of level ground to plant their crops. Inca farmers had no animals to help them so everything was done by hand. They grew maize, potatoes, beans, cotton, and chili peppers. Farmers also kept **llamas** and **alpacas** for their wool. Ducks and

The road network allowed merchants to transport produce from the terraces where the farmers grew their crops.

guinea pigs were raised for food.

Produce was sent all over the Inca empire by the network of roads. Fish from the sea and fruits from the jungle were also distributed along these routes.

The Inca farmers used a foot plow called a chaki taklla to dig furrows in the soil.

17

CHILDREN WERE NAMED AT 12

In the first two years of its life a baby was called baby. They were washed every morning in cold water and often left to play in a hole dug in the ground while the mother worked. At around three to four years old they were given a temporary name. Peasant children began doing chores at an early age. Sons of nobles had tutors to teach them laws, politics, and military ways.

A local priest oversees the marriage ceremony of a 12-year-old girl and a 24-year-old man as they exchange sandals.

At around 11 to 12 years old boys were given a name. They were regarded as adults at 14. Girls were named at the same age as boys and were married soon after.

Boys were married at 24. Their wives were chosen for them by the local governor. At 25 boys started to pay labor tax and did military service.

The State Provided for All

 Everybody had to work. People farmed the land that was allotted to them as well as the lands of the Sapa Inca and the **Sun god**'s land. Men also had to serve time in the army and work on community projects such as building bridges and roads. Some of the food and clothing that the people paid to the Sapa Inca was put into storehouses.

*Using a **quipu**, an official records an elderly woman's food and clothing which was supplied by the state's storehouse.*

When people reached 60 years of age they were expected only to do light duties. At 80 years old they could have food and clothing from the state's storehouses.

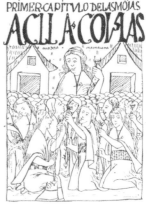

The state decided women's careers. At 10 years old they were chosen as priestesses or servants to the Sapa Inca. If not, they stayed in their villages as peasants.

PUNISHMENTS WERE VERY HARSH

When people committed a crime it was considered a crime against the Sapa Inca and so punishments were harsh. There were no prisons. The death penalty was given for murder, stealing, breaking into the state storage rooms, and laziness. The death penalty could be carried out by hanging, stoning, or pushing off a cliff.

22

A man condemned to death is pushed off a cliff as officials and family members witness the execution.

For first offenses a punishment might be less harsh. Public humiliation was common. Offenders might have to sit by the city gate or in the **plaza**, and tell people about their crime.

Upper classes were punished more severely than the common people as they were expected to know better.

THE INCAS WERE VERY CREATIVE

Most people did some type of craftwork. Cloth-making was the most important craft. Llama wool was coarse and greasy and was used to make blankets, sacks, and rope. Alpaca wool was most commonly used to make clothing. The finest cloth was made from **vicuña** wool which was soft and silky. Much of the wool was dyed before spinning it.

24

*Women weave patterned cloth on **back looms** as young girls store and spin wool. Behind, a boy leads llamas in to be sheared.*

The Incas were skilled potters. Pots were made by coiling lengths of clay into a pot shape and smoothing the sides. They were often decorated with colorful geometric patterns.

Hundreds of tons of gold and silver were mined each year. Skilled goldsmiths in Cuzco worked the precious metals into beautiful objects.

INCA PRIESTS ALSO ACTED AS DOCTORS

Priests and priestesses carried out religious ceremonies which were very important to the Incas. Religion was so much part of everyday life that there were more priests than soldiers. The official state religion was Sun worship. The High Priests of the Sun were the most important and they had great power and influence at the Inca court.

*A priest cuts a hole in the skull of a patient (known as **trepanning**) as others hold him down.*

Many Inca priests were also doctors and could cure serious illnesses such as **dysentery**, ulcers and eye problems. There were also priest surgeons who amputated limbs and performed brain surgery.

*Surgeon-priests anesthetized their patients by giving them **coca** leaves to chew.*

THE INCA EMPIRE WAS DESTROYED IN 1572

In November 1532, a new Sapa Inca, Atahualpa, won a great victory against his brother's forces. He ended a civil war that had cost thousands of lives. Close by was a small band of 177 Spanish **conquistadors** led by Francisco Pizarro. He sent a message to Atahualpa requesting a meeting. The Sapa Inca arrived the next day with unarmed attendants.

The Sapa Inca, Atahualpa, is grabbed by Pizarro as his unarmed bodyguards are cut down in an ambush in Cajamarca.

Pizarro had laid an ambush and the unarmed Incas were slaughtered. Atahualpa was captured. Without their leader the Incas did nothing to retaliate.

After receiving gold and silver as ransom, Pizarro had Atahualpa killed. By 1541 the Spanish were quarreling and Pizarro was assassinated. The last Inca stronghold was conquered in 1572 and Inca ways were stamped out.

GLOSSARY

alpaca
A domesticated member of the camel family that lives in South America.

back loom
A weaving device that is attached at one end to a pole and at the other end to the weaver by means of a strap around the waist.

coca
A plant grown in South America whose leaves, when chewed, suppress hunger, thirst, pain, and fatigue.

conquistador
A Spanish soldier or explorer who sailed beyond Europe to the Americas, conquering territory and opening trade routes.

dysentery
An inflammation of the intestine caused by contaminated food and water.

llama
A domesticated member of the camel family used as a source of wool, meat, and as a pack animal by Andean peoples.

mace
A club-like weapon with a heavy head attached to a handle. It is used to deliver powerful blows against an opponent.

mortar
A paste used to bind together building blocks such as stones and bricks.

mummification
Preservation of the body after a person has died. Incas sometimes treated the corpses with alcohol before wrapping them in layers of cloth. More often they were left in deserts or at a high altitude where the dry, cold air preserved the corpse naturally.

plaza
An open public space, such as a town square.

quipu
A device made of many colored strings that were knotted and used by the Incas to record information from tax to census records.

Sapa Inca
Meaning "the only Inca," he was the Inca emperor and regarded as a descendant of the Sun god.

Sun god
Known as "Inti," the ancient Inca Sun god was worshiped by everybody in the Inca empire.

suspension bridge
A type of bridge that has cables or ropes suspended between towers, from which vertical suspenders attach to the deck below.

trepanning
A surgical operation in which a hole is drilled or scraped into the human skull.

vicuña
A small relative of the llama that produces small amounts of extremely fine wool. The wool is highly prized because the animal can only be shorn once every three years.

INDEX

FOR MORE INFORMATION

BOOKS

DK Publishing. *DK Eyewitness Books: Aztec, Inca & Maya.* London: Penguin, 2011.

Evans, Callum. *The Fun Bits of History You Don't Know about Incas.* Seattle: CreateSpace Independent, 2015.

WEBSITES

Kids Konnect – Ancient Inca Facts
kidskonnect.com/history/ancient-inca/

Ducksters – Aztecs, Maya, Inca
www.ducksters.com/history/aztec_maya_inca.php